# Clo Security & Compliance

for
dummies®
A Wiley Brand

# Cloud Security & Compliance

Palo Alto Networks® Special Edition

## by Lawrence Miller, CISSP

## Cloud Security & Compliance For Dummies®, Palo Alto Networks® Special Edition

Published by
**John Wiley & Sons, Inc.**
111 River St.
Hoboken, NJ 07030-5774
www.wiley.com

For general information on our other products and services, or how to create a custom *For Dummies* book for your business or organization, please contact our Business Development Department in the U.S. at 877-409-4177, contact info@dummies.biz, or visit www.wiley.com/go/custompub. For information about licensing the *For Dummies* brand for products or services, contact BrandedRights&Licenses@Wiley.com.

ISBN 978-1-119-54549-1 (pbk); ISBN 978-1-119-54551-4 (ebk)

Manufactured in the United States of America

V10004778_092618

## Publisher's Acknowledgments

Some of the people who helped bring this book to market include the following:

**Project Editor:** Elizabeth Kuball

**Acquisitions Editor:** Katie Mohr

**Editorial Manager:** Rev Mengle

**Business Development Representative:** Karen Hattan

**Production Editor:** Tamilmani Varadharaj

**Special Help:** Michaline Todd, Janet Matsuda, Shanta Kohli, Stephanie Williams, Anuj Sawani, Chris Morosco, Sheiley Asana, Matt Keil, Tim Prendergast, Sai Balabhadrapatruni, Alison Arnott

# Table of Contents

# Introduction

Today, digital technology defines the competitive battleground, and organizations are constantly striving to improve their services with new applications. These organizations are rapidly adopting cloud technologies to keep pace with growing business demands and take advantage of efficiencies and scalability in the cloud. As a result, the traditional corporate perimeter is fading, and mobile workers are driving ever-increasing usage of SaaS applications. Organizations today are using a mix of private and public cloud services to gain the cost savings, agility, and speed benefits of the cloud.

As a result of this digital transformation, risk management and data protection are top concerns for organizations migrating to the cloud. IT leaders worry about securing the business. Whether on-premises, in the cloud, or mobile, the entire IT architecture must be secure to preserve the integrity and longevity of the business. Legacy security tools, policies, and processes designed for traditional data centers and IT operations cannot adapt to address SaaS applications or the continuous deployment model and pace of change in the cloud. Although many tools are available for securing the cloud — including native security services from public cloud providers — siloed security products, manual operations, and human errors continue to slow down the business and create risk. Visibility and control in the cloud are challenging, and cloud environments are complex.

To be successful, organizations need a consistent approach to security that spans all of their operating environments, from on-premises data centers to multiple public and private clouds. They need tools and processes that simplify operations through automation driven by machine learning and analytics, and cross-platform capabilities that prevent data breaches across the cloud, data center, and endpoints.

# About This Book

*Cloud Security & Compliance For Dummies* consists of six chapters that explore

>> The evolution of cloud computing and cloud security (Chapter 1)

>> How to secure the cloud in your organization (Chapter 2)

>> The regulatory landscape in the cloud (Chapter 3)

>> How to build an effective cybersecurity team and leverage automation in the cloud (Chapter 4)

>> Coming trends in cloud security (Chapter 5)

>> Best practice recommendations for securing the cloud (Chapter 6)

Finally, if you get lost in all the acronyms and technical terms used throughout the book, there's a glossary in the back of the book to help you out!

# Foolish Assumptions

It's been said that most assumptions have outlived their useless-ness, but I'll assume a few things nonetheless:

>> You're a chief information officer (CIO), chief technology officer (CTO), chief information security officer (CISO), cloud architect, IT compliance and risk manager, network practitioner, or a security practitioner.

>> You have a general understanding of cloud computing and how it supports business agility in your organization.

>> You need to better understand the scope and breakdown of cloud risks and how to deploy security in a frictionless manner to prevent data breaches without negatively impacting your business and development needs — today and in the future.

If any of these assumptions describes you, then this book is for you! If none of these assumptions describes you, keep reading anyway. It's a great book and when you finish reading it, you'll know quite a bit about cloud security and compliance.

# Icons Used in This Book

Throughout this book, I use special icons to call attention to important information. Here's what to expect:

**REMEMBER**

This icon points out information that you should commit to your nonvolatile memory, your gray matter, or your noggin — along with anniversaries and birthdays!

**TIP**

Tips are appreciated, never expected — and I sure hope you'll appreciate these useful nuggets of information. This icon points out useful nuggets of information.

**WARNING**

This icon points out the stuff your mother warned you about. Okay, probably not. But you should take heed nonetheless — you may just save yourself some time and frustration!

# Beyond the Book

There's only so much I can cover in 72 short pages, so if you find yourself at the end of this book, thinking, "Gosh, this was an amazing book! Where can I learn more?," just go to www.paloaltonetworks.com/products/secure-the-cloud.

# Where to Go from Here

If you don't know where you're going, any chapter will get you there — but Chapter 1 might be a good place to start! However, if you see a particular topic that piques your interest, feel free to jump ahead to that chapter. Each chapter is written to stand on its own, so feel free to start reading anywhere and skip around to your heart's content! Read this book in any order that suits you (though I don't recommend upside down or sideways).

# Chapter **1**

# Understanding the Evolution of the Cloud and Its Impact on Security

I n this chapter, you learn the basics of cloud computing and how to assess your organization's cloud maturity level. You also look at how risk has evolved in the cloud and what the shared responsibility model means for your organization.

## Defining Different Cloud Types

It seems as though the cloud is everywhere today. But to ensure we're on the same page when talking about the cloud, let's start on page one by defining a common cloud lexicon with some help from our friends at the U.S. National Institute of Standards and Technology (NIST).

In *Special Publication 800-145*, NIST defines the following five essential characteristics of cloud computing:

>> **On-demand self-service:** "A consumer can unilaterally provision computing capabilities, such as server time and network storage, as needed automatically without requiring human interaction with each service provider."

>> **Broad network access:** "Capabilities are available over the network and accessed through standard mechanisms that promote use by heterogeneous thin or thick client platforms (for example, mobile phones, tablets, laptops, and workstations)."

>> **Resource pooling:** "The provider's computing resources are pooled to serve multiple consumers using a multi-tenant model, with different physical and virtual resources dynamically assigned and reassigned according to consumer demand. Examples of resources include storage, processing, memory, and network bandwidth."

>> **Rapid elasticity:** "Capabilities can be elastically provisioned and released, in some cases automatically, to scale rapidly outward and inward commensurate with demand. To the consumer, the capabilities available for provisioning often appear to be unlimited and can be appropriated in any quantity at any time."

>> **Measured service:** "Cloud systems automatically control and optimize resource use by leveraging a metering capability at some level of abstraction appropriate to the type of service (for example, storage, processing, bandwidth, and active user accounts). Resource usage can be monitored, controlled, and reported, providing transparency for both the provider and consumer of the utilized service."

NIST defines the following four cloud deployment models (although community clouds are not that common):

>> **Private cloud:** "The cloud infrastructure is provisioned for exclusive use by a single organization comprising multiple consumers (for example, business units). It may be owned, managed, and operated by the organization, a third party, or some combination of them, and it may exist on or off premises."

>> **Community cloud:** "The cloud infrastructure is provisioned for exclusive use by a specific community of consumers from organizations that have shared concerns (for example, mission, security requirements, policy, and compliance considerations). It may be owned, managed, and operated by one or more of the organizations in the community, a third party, or some combination of them, and it may exist on or off premises."

>> **Public cloud:** "The cloud infrastructure is provisioned for open use by the general public. It may be owned, managed, and operated by a business, academic, or government organization, or some combination of them. It exists on the premises of the cloud provider."

>> **Hybrid cloud:** "The cloud infrastructure is a composition of two or more distinct cloud infrastructures (private, community, or public) that remain unique entities, but are bound together by standardized or proprietary technology that enables data and application portability (for example, cloud bursting for load balancing between clouds)."

Finally, NIST defines the following three cloud computing service models:

>> **Software as a Service (SaaS):** "The capability provided to the consumer is to use the provider's applications running on a cloud infrastructure. The applications are accessible from various client devices through either a thin client interface, such as a web browser (for example, web-based email), or a program interface. The consumer does not manage or control the underlying cloud infrastructure including network, servers, operating systems, storage, or even individual application capabilities, with the possible exception of limited user-specific application configuration settings."

>> **Platform as a Service (PaaS):** "The capability provided to the consumer is to deploy onto the cloud infrastructure consumer-created or acquired applications created using programming languages, libraries, services, and tools supported by the provider. The consumer does not manage or control the underlying cloud infrastructure including network, servers, operating systems, or storage, but has control over the deployed applications and possibly configuration settings for the application-hosting environment."

>> **Infrastructure as a Service (IaaS):** "The capability provided to the consumer is to provision processing, storage, networks, and other fundamental computing resources where the consumer is able to deploy and run arbitrary software, which can include operating systems and applications. The consumer does not manage or control the underlying cloud infrastructure but has control over operating systems, storage, and deployed applications; and possibly limited control of select networking components (for example, host firewalls)."

Now that we're speaking the same language with regard to the cloud, let's take a look at cloud maturity in your organization.

# Assessing the Cloud Maturity of Your Organization

Ironically, although the cloud is everywhere, many organizations make the mistake of treating the cloud as a separate, isolated environment when it comes to security and compliance. A siloed security approach, using multiple security tools from different vendors to solve for narrow use cases, results in a fragmented security environment in which IT teams must manually correlate data to implement actionable protections. This does not scale when battling cyber adversaries who use automation to wage sophisticated attacks at higher and higher volumes. If your security ecosystem is unable to inform or collaborate with other products, let alone automatically coordinate or communicate with other capabilities in the network, your organization is forced to rely on your least-scalable resource to fight machine-generated attacks: people.

Knowing your organization's cloud maturity level is an important first step in creating an effective strategy for security and compliance in the cloud. The following cloud maturity model defines three stages of maturity, based on an organization's level of cloud adoption:

>> **Cloud evaluators (beginner):** In this stage, organizations are exploring cloud technologies and options to prioritize which applications to deploy in the cloud. Line of business teams are often experimenting with cloud technologies, while the organization as a whole is still working to define its cloud policy and best practices. Security teams pilot

approaches and converge with application development teams for deployment.

>> **Cloud implementers (intermediate):** Organizations in this stage have moved production workloads to the cloud (utilizing either hybrid cloud or single cloud architectures). There is collaboration among teams to formalize and implement cloud policy and deployment best practices, including building out automated DevOps workflows. Security and application development teams work together throughout the development and deployment process.

>> **Cloud optimizers (advanced):** At this stage, the organization's digital transformation depends on the cloud, and the cloud is used for business-critical workloads. The organization may be utilizing multiple cloud ecosystems, each for specific business imperatives. There is a strategic business initiative around broadening and automating cloud policy and processes around operations, security, and compliance.

The RightScale *2018 State of the Cloud Report* found that 81 percent of enterprises have a multi-cloud (multiple public, multiple private, or hybrid) strategy, leveraging five clouds on average. According to the report, the top five cloud challenges for organizations depend on their level of cloud maturity, as shown in Table 1-1.

**TABLE 1-1** Top Five Cloud Challenges Based on Cloud Maturity Level

| Order | Beginner | Intermediate | Advanced |
|---|---|---|---|
| First | Security (85 percent) | Managing costs (80 percent) | Managing costs (77 percent) |
| Second | Lack of resources and expertise (82 percent) | Security (78 percent) | Security (77 percent) |
| Third | Managing costs (80 percent) | Lack of resources and expertise (78 percent) | Compliance (73 percent) |
| Fourth | Governance and control (75 percent) | Governance and control (76 percent) | Governance and control (70 percent) |
| Fifth | Compliance (74 percent) | Compliance (69 percent) | Lack of resources and expertise (67 percent) |

*Source: RightScale 2018 State of the Cloud Report*

**TIP**

Start by assessing your organization's cloud maturity level to help prioritize your cloud challenges and create an appropriate cloud strategy.

**REMEMBER**

To successfully secure their organization, security teams must have consistent visibility and control across their entire environment, including on-premises data centers, private and public clouds, and endpoints. They need security tools, processes, and policies that enable effective cross-platform detect, prevent, and response capabilities. This visibility and control can be accomplished by leveraging automation, driven by analytics and machine learning, to keep up with the speed and scale of complex, multi-cloud and on-premises environments.

# Looking at the Evolution of Risk in the Cloud

As more organizations move critical workloads to the public cloud, IT must be vigilant about the security of systems, data, and services in the cloud. Many cloud customers, especially DevOps teams and individual business groups, often mistakenly assume that the cloud is inherently secure. This mistake frequently exposes organizations to greater risk in the cloud.

The Cybersecurity Insiders *2018 Cloud Security Report* found that 18 percent of organizations had experienced a cloud security incident in the past 12 months, and another 18 percent were unsure if they had experienced an incident. The top cloud security challenges cited by cybersecurity professionals in the report included

>> Data loss/leakage (67 percent)

>> Threats to data privacy (61 percent)

>> Breaches of confidentiality (53 percent)

What are the root causes of these disturbing trends? There are many opportunities for cloud evaluators to unwittingly introduce new risks — such as data leaks due to incorrect use of SaaS apps and improperly configured access rights. Security teams have less visibility and control when users access SaaS applications and developers deploy workloads in the public cloud, particularly when deployments use PaaS.

Much of the risk in the cloud is due to the fact that data and applications in the cloud are literally everywhere. This is particularly true for organizations without a well-defined cloud strategy. These organizations may not have selected a set of sanctioned SaaS applications that can be secured effectively. Without guidance, employees adopt innovative apps with the potential for improved productivity, but without fully understanding the associated risks. Unfortunately, it's hostile territory full of cybercriminals ready to take advantage of unsuspecting users who may accidentally misconfigure permissions in a file sharing service. Users also make mistakes or use poor judgment when sharing files. All of these risks can expose sensitive data.

The move to cloud is enabling many organizations to adopt a more agile, iterative application development methodology. In so doing, developers and their workloads need rapid and oftentimes automated, yet secure access to web-based resources like GitHub, Yum, apt-get, and OS update mechanisms for Windows or Linux.

Developers are regularly accessing web-based resources — executables, how-to guides, and workbooks of all types — to get their jobs done more quickly and effectively. These same web resources are commonly used by attackers to inject malware into an unsuspecting network. In 2017, security incidents involving two commonly used development apps — MongoDB and Elasticsearch — were discovered. In the case of MongoDB, older, unpatched versions were compromised, exposing users' personal data. The Elasticsearch incident found that some 4,000 or so instances were distributing malware. Here are some more recent examples:

>> Malware was discovered in at least three Arch Linux packages available on Arch User Repository (AUR), the official Arch Linux repository of user-submitted packages.

>> A cryptocurrency miner was found hidden in the source code of an Ubuntu snap package hosted on the official Ubuntu Snap Store.

>> A joint report published by threat intelligence firms Digital Shadows and Onapsis warned of increased attacks on enterprise resource planning (ERP) systems such as SAP and Oracle.

Monolithic architectures that worked in on-premises environments are inefficient in the cloud. A service-oriented architecture (SOA) enables agility and scalability in the cloud. Microservices are a variant of SOA in which an application is composed of a collection of loosely coupled, modular services. Containers (discussed in Chapter 2), are increasingly popular among developers as a preferred technology for efficiently deploying microservices, and more than ever, these technologies are being used side by side. According to a recent Cloud Foundry Foundation study, 77 percent of IT decision makers reported using or evaluating Platform as a Service (PaaS), 72 percent are using or evaluating container technologies, and 46 percent are using or evaluating serverless computing. More than a third (39 percent) are using a combination of all three technologies together.

Lack of visibility in IaaS and PaaS environments further exposes organizations to risk in the cloud. Lateral (east–west) movement in the data center — including cloud data centers — by an attacker can go undetected indefinitely without complete visibility and controls to restrict lateral movement. Without visibility, you also run the risk of not detecting unauthorized users who deploy cloud resources for cryptocurrency mining or other purposes, at your cost.

Finally, there is often a misconception by organizations that security in the cloud is the responsibility of the cloud provider. However, cloud providers are responsible for security *of* the cloud — the customer is always responsible for the security of their workloads, services, and data *in* the cloud. This is known as the shared responsibility model (see the next section).

# Understanding the Shared Responsibility Model

Cloud-based applications and the data that go with them are becoming increasingly distributed among varying environments to improve the agility of the organization and reduce costs. These environments include private clouds, public clouds (hybrid or dedicated), and Software as a Service (SaaS) applications, each bringing its own unique agility benefits and security issues.

The concern over data exposure has made cloud security a priority. The challenge has become balancing the organization's need for agility while improving the security of applications and securing the data as it moves between the various clouds. Gaining visibility and preventing attacks that are attempting to exfiltrate data, both from an external location and through a lateral attack, becomes imperative across all the locations where the applications and data reside.

A number of different groups within an organization could be responsible for cloud security: the network team, security team, apps team, compliance team, or infrastructure team. However, cloud security is also a shared responsibility between the cloud vendor and the organization:

>> **Private:** Enterprises are responsible for all aspects of security for the cloud as it's hosted within their own data centers. This includes the physical network, infrastructure, hypervisor, virtual network, operating systems, firewalls, service configuration, identity and access management, and so on. The enterprise also owns the data and the security of the data.

>> **Public:** In public clouds, like Amazon Web Services (AWS), Google Cloud, or Microsoft Azure, the cloud vendor owns the infrastructure, physical network, and hypervisor. The enterprise owns the workload operating system (OS), apps, virtual network, access to their tenant environment/account, and data.

>> **SaaS:** SaaS vendors are primarily responsible for the security of their platform, which includes physical security, infrastructure, and application security. These vendors do not own the customer data or assume responsibility for how customers use the applications. As such, the enterprise is responsible for security that would prevent and minimize the risk of malicious data exfiltration, accidental exposure, or malware insertion.

As companies transition from private to public cloud, or to SaaS applications, the responsibility for securing data, apps, and infrastructure falls less in the hands of the enterprise and more into the hands of the vendor (see Figure 1-1). However, regardless of the platform used, the enterprise will always be responsible for ensuring the security and privacy of its own data.

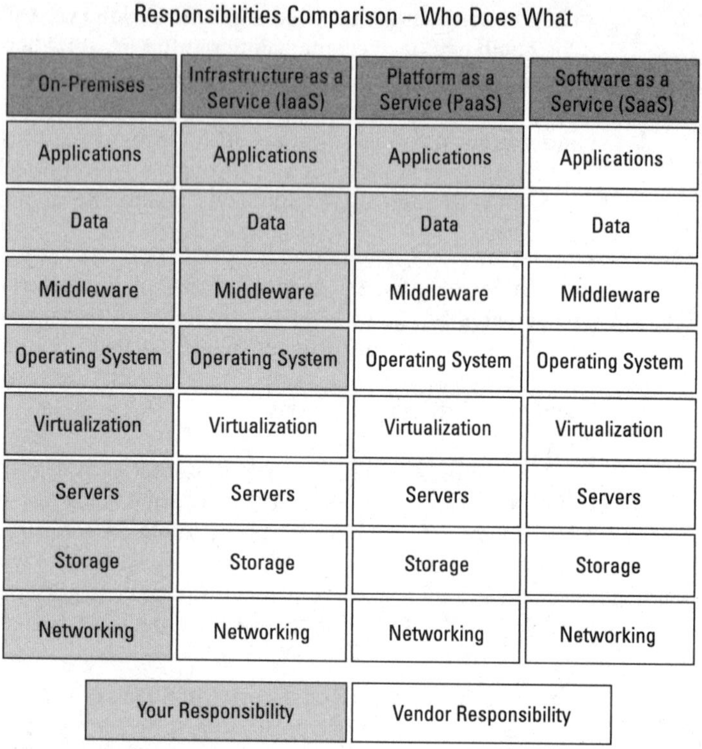

Responsibilities Comparison – Who Does What

| On-Premises | Infrastructure as a Service (IaaS) | Platform as a Service (PaaS) | Software as a Service (SaaS) |
|---|---|---|---|
| Applications | Applications | Applications | Applications |
| Data | Data | Data | Data |
| Middleware | Middleware | Middleware | Middleware |
| Operating System | Operating System | Operating System | Operating System |
| Virtualization | Virtualization | Virtualization | Virtualization |
| Servers | Servers | Servers | Servers |
| Storage | Storage | Storage | Storage |
| Networking | Networking | Networking | Networking |

| Your Responsibility | Vendor Responsibility |
|---|---|

**FIGURE 1-1:** Cloud security is a shared responsibility.

In order to keep applications and data secure, IT security must clearly understand where cloud vendors' security responsibilities end and where theirs begin. To ensure they're fulfilling their security responsibilities as part of the shared responsibility model, organizations must have the right tools. These tools must provide visibility into activity within the cloud application, detailed analytics on usage to prevent data risk and compliance violations, context-aware policy controls to drive enforcement and remediate if a violation occurs, and real-time threat intelligence on known and unknown threats to detect and prevent new malware insertion points.

IN THIS CHAPTER

» Establishing clearly defined responsibilities in your organization

» Knowing your potential risks in the cloud

» Recognizing the limitations of existing tools

» Creating a secure multi-cloud strategy

» Implementing cloud security best practices

# Chapter **2**

# Getting Started with Cloud Security in Your Organization

I n this chapter, you look at individual cloud security responsibilities that need to be defined in your organization; learn how to assess risk in the cloud; examine existing cloud security tools; learn what it takes to create a secure cloud strategy for Infrastructure as a Service (IaaS), Platform as a Service (PaaS), Software as a Service (SaaS), multi-cloud, and container environments; and explore security best practices for the cloud.

## Defining Organizational Cloud Security Responsibilities

Beyond the shared responsibility model (discussed in Chapter 1), it's important to define individual responsibilities for cloud security within your organization and ensure everyone knows what is required. It's not enough — and even a bit of a cliché — to simply say, "Security is everyone's responsibility."

Beginning at the top, executive sponsorship is key. Fortunately, in today's regulatory landscape (discussed in Chapter 3), executive sponsorship is practically mandated. The potential financial impact to a business of regulatory noncompliance can be as devastating as (or worse than) a data breach itself. Beyond the financial penalties, many regulations carry criminal penalties for business executives and other fiduciaries of a business.

TIP

Instead of treating cloud security as a stand-alone policy, the enterprise security strategy should encompass the entire environment, including on-premises data centers and public and private clouds. This strategy should reduce overall complexity with a consistent approach that leverages automation driven by analytics across the environment.

So, what does executive sponsorship look like? It begins with leading by example. Executives must not only talk the talk, they must walk the walk. If corporate policy, for example, requires corporate data on mobile devices to be encrypted and access to SaaS applications need multi-factor authentication (MFA), then "one-off" exceptions shouldn't be made for executives. Beyond leading by example, executives need to ensure that security and compliance initiatives have the appropriate support and resources, and that the impact of strategic business decisions on the overall security and compliance posture of the organization is always considered.

Security and compliance teams must define and enforce appropriate policies that securely enable the business. To be effective, security and compliance teams must understand and align with business goals and objectives, and they must not be a bottleneck to productivity and efficiency.

Line-of-business managers have a responsibility to ensure that the organization's cloud security and compliance governance is understood and adhered to within their respective areas of the business. As business needs evolve, line-of-business managers should partner with security teams to evaluate the risk versus return of adopting new tools. Circumventing a security policy, such as a requirement to use only sanctioned SaaS applications, to achieve a short-term business objective or productivity goal should never be acceptable. Instead, the security tools should adapt to the business need and drive the desired user behavior.

Working with security and compliance teams also helps to ensure that individual lines of business are able to take advantage of any current relationships the organization may have with vendors or cloud providers to procure services more economically and get support quickly when it's needed, instead of operating in a vacuum with siloed cloud solutions.

DevOps teams are under constant pressure to deliver software projects and updates quickly and reduce time to market. To meet these demands, security requirements must be defined and understood at the beginning of any project and ideally integrated into the application delivery workflow. In this way, development teams can continue moving forward without frequently having to stop and reset to address security vulnerabilities and compliance violations.

Finally, individual end users have a responsibility to follow corporate governance with respect to cloud security and compliance. They must understand the inherent risks in the cloud and safeguard the data to which they have been entrusted as if it were their own personal data.

# Assessing Risk in the Cloud

To properly assess risk in the cloud, organizations should apply any internal risk assessment processes to their cloud deployments.

Additionally, consider using a risk assessment framework, such as the Cloud Security Alliance (CSA) Cloud Controls Matrix (CCM). The CCM consists of 16 domains that describe cloud security principles and best practices to help organizations assess the overall security risk of a cloud provider. The 16 domains are as follows:

>> Application and interface security

>> Audit assurance and compliance

>> Business continuity management and operational resilience

>> Change control and configuration management

>> Data security and information life-cycle management

>> Data center security

>> Encryption and key management

- » Governance and risk management
- » Human resources
- » Identity and access management
- » Infrastructure and virtualization security
- » Interoperability and portability
- » Mobile security
- » Security incident management, e-discovery, and cloud forensics
- » Supply chain management, transparency, and accountability
- » Threat and vulnerability management

The CCM also maps individual cloud controls to relevant data protection/information security regulations and standards such as the American Institute of Certified Public Accountants (AICPA), Service Organization Control (SOC 2), Canada Personal Information Protection and Electronic Documents Act (PIPEDA), International Organization for Standardization (ISO) 27001/27002/27017/27018, U.S. Health Insurance Portability and Accountability Act (HIPAA), Payment Card Industry Data Security Standard (PCI DSS), and many more.

TIP

The Consensus Assessments Initiative Questionnaire (CAIQ) is a questionnaire consisting of nearly 300 questions across all 16 of the CCM domains to help you assess the risk of your organization and your cloud providers. Go to `https://cloudsecurity alliance.org` to download a free copy of the questionnaire.

# Evaluating Existing Security Tools

There are several security options to choose from when moving to the cloud. However, the approaches widely used today have proven insufficient in providing the holistic view of the cloud required to detect and prevent advanced threats and data breaches. I cover these approaches in the following sections.

## Native public cloud security

Cloud security is a shared responsibility between the cloud provider and the customer. In IaaS, customers are responsible for protecting their applications and data running within the public cloud, whereas in SaaS, they're responsible solely for the security of their data. To aid with protection, cloud service providers offer basic native security services, including access controls and data protection tools. However, the level of security provided by these native security services doesn't meet the requirements of the enterprise and is limited to only that cloud provider. For example, these services leverage tools that are focused on controlling access based on port information (using access control lists [ACLs] and port-based firewalls) or only inspect a small set of applications (using web application firewalls [WAFs]), and are unable to prevent advanced threats and data exfiltration. Fragmented security and complex management overhead often results because organizations tend to use IaaS, PaaS, and SaaS offerings from multiple cloud vendors. Therefore, organizations must complement these native security services with additional enterprise security tools and services of their own.

## Point products

Using multiple security tools from multiple vendors to solve for specific use cases results in a fragmented security environment in which IT teams must manually correlate data to implement actionable security protections. This level of human intervention increases the likelihood for human error, leaving organizations exposed to threats and data breaches. For example, cloud access security brokers (CASBs) are useful to mitigate risks within SaaS environments. Instead of adding another point security tool that increases operational complexity, CASB capabilities should be part of a broader cybersecurity platform.

## Legacy network and content security

Legacy security vendors claim to offer an adequate level of protection to secure your cloud environments. However, what they refer to is often a virtualized instance of hardware placed in the public cloud. This approach is not truly cloud-integrated security, negating the on-demand nature of the cloud and agility benefits. Plus, it lacks the automation required to enable consistent, frictionless security across your entire multi-cloud environment.

# Building a Security Strategy

Ideally, security should speed application development and business growth while preventing data loss and business downtime. Your security vendor should use the same technologies you're using to deliver services to customers:

>> **Security delivered as a service** to ensure consistent protection across locations and clouds with an agile, scalable ecosystem

>> **Analytics** to confidently automate prevention and prioritize your business

>> **Automation** to bridge the cybersecurity skills gap by turning threat detection into prevention, adapting to dynamic environments through context-based access policies, and accelerating response using analytics and machine learning

REMEMBER

Cloud vendors will profess that their security is better than yours (and it likely is), but attackers don't care where your data is located. They have one goal in mind: to compromise your network, navigate to a target (be it data, intellectual property, or compute resources), and execute their end goal.

To minimize business disruption, organizations must protect their cloud assets. With today's sophisticated attacks, advanced enterprise-grade security is the only way to prevent successful breaches. More important, security capabilities must protect the entire IT environment, including multi-cloud environments (private clouds, IaaS, PaaS, and SaaS), as well as the organization's data centers and mobile users, using a consistent frictionless approach.

## IaaS and PaaS security requirements

Many organizations will transition to the cloud following a "lift and shift" methodology that moves their enterprise applications directly to IaaS using only foundational components — compute, network, and storage. Over time, those same organizations began building applications that leverage cloud efficiencies. Now, applications consume multiple components from IaaS and PaaS services (see Figure 2-1). PaaS offerings significantly reduce development time and allow apps to scale efficiently based on demand.

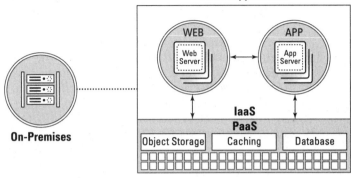

**FIGURE 2-1:** Application development in IaaS and PaaS.

To provide the enterprise-level security required for applications within IaaS and PaaS environments, a multidimensional approach is needed, including in-line, API-based and, host-based protection components (see Figure 2-2):

- » **In-line:** Protect and segment cloud workloads to safeguard against internal and external threats. By investigating communications in your cloud environment, you'll gain application-level visibility into north–south traffic flowing in and out of your cloud environment, as well as east–west traffic between workloads. Segmentation policies ensure appropriate levels of interaction between various cloud workloads, such as web applications and database workloads.

- » **API-based:** Provide continuous discovery and monitoring, compliance reporting, and data security. The API-based approach is transparent to developers and enables security teams to discover and monitor cloud resources and assets for any suspicious activity, secure storage services by preventing misconfigurations, and comply with industry standards (such as CSA CCM, ISO 27017/27018, PCI DSS, and SOC 2), as well as regulations (such as GDPR, HIPAA, NIS, PIPEDA, and SOX) with customizable reports and controls.

- » **Host-based:** Secure the operating system and applications within workloads. A lightweight host agent deployed within the cloud instance detects any zero-day exploits and ensures the integrity of the operating system and applications. As attackers uncover vulnerabilities, the agent-based approach can provide protection until organizations are able to patch components.

To provide a consistent, frictionless security approach throughout multi-cloud infrastructure, security should use automation to become part of the development process. Developers do not need to be security experts so long as automated, consistent protections can be inserted into the environment. In addition, it's critical to understand that security requirements for IaaS and PaaS must be delivered through a consistent security approach that supports applications and data across the three major cloud service platforms: Amazon Web Services (AWS), Microsoft Azure, and Google Cloud Platform (GCP).

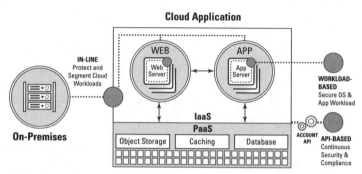

**FIGURE 2-2:** Critical cloud protections for IaaS and PaaS.

# SaaS security requirements

SaaS applications have changed the way organizations do business, in many cases, leading the way in "cloud first" directives. Benefits aside, they've also introduced new security risks in the process, including malware propagation across the network and sensitive data exposure, often resulting from uncontrolled SaaS application usage or misconfigurations. The push to address these security gaps led to the creation of the CASB category.

The following are the deployment modes by which to deliver CASB functions, along with additional recommendations to ensure comprehensive security for your SaaS applications and data (see Figure 2-3):

> » **In-line deployment** provides SaaS application usage visibility and granular, real-time policy enforcement. Through in-line protection provided by cloud-based security services or hardware or virtual appliances, organizations can understand SaaS usage across your users, and build policy to control your

risk exposure accordingly. Policies can also be enforced when unmanaged devices access sanctioned SaaS applications. This helps prevent exfiltration of sensitive data across all cloud applications.

>> **API deployment** provides deeper protections for sanctioned, enterprise-approved applications and performs several functions, including data leak prevention for all data at rest in the cloud application or service, as well as ongoing monitoring of user activity and administrative configurations.

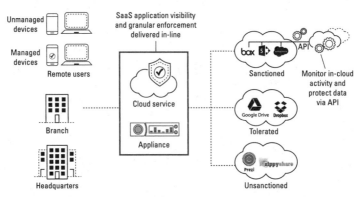

**FIGURE 2-3:** SaaS security approaches.

In the same way, IaaS and PaaS cloud components must be secured, SaaS applications, such as Box, Dropbox, GitHub, Google Drive, Office 365, and Salesforce, must also be protected using consistent policy enforcement, regardless of application and cloud provider.

# Multi-cloud security requirements

Enterprise data and applications now frequently reside in a multitude of cloud environments, including private and public clouds, spanning IaaS, PaaS, and SaaS.

Despite this momentum, several barriers still slow adoption, and security remains a top concern. Also, although native public cloud security controls provide some degree of access control and identity management, breaches are often the result of improper use, misconfigurations, or advanced threats. Confidently accelerating the move to the cloud requires consistent, automated protections across multi-cloud deployments that prevent data loss and business downtime.

# MICROSERVICES ARCHITECTURE AND CONTAINER SECURITY

Microservices architectures (discussed in Chapter 1) and container technologies, such as Docker, Kubernetes, Mesosphere, and OpenShift, are enabling new application architectures for legacy apps, refactored apps, and microservices, among others. Containers are popular among DevOps teams, in particular, because they provide a fast and relatively easy way to quickly deploy new application workloads in a self-contained "infrastructure as code" package that enables standardization, portability, efficiency, and scalability.

However, these new application architectures also introduce new attack vectors including control plane attacks against the orchestrator, network-based attacks across the infrastructure, container registry attacks, and host operating system attacks (see the figure).

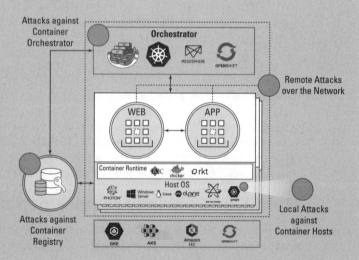

Current approaches toward securing container infrastruture are insufficient. These include built-in container security that is immature and ineffective, container security point products that have limited scope and do not address the security needs of hybrid applications that use containers and virtual machines, and legacy network security tools that negate the value of containers.

To properly secure container environments, organizations need to deploy in-line network protections and host operating system security and API-based continuous monitoring and compliance checks. These security tools enable breach prevention, registry scanning, and orchestrator protections for information assurance, assessment, and monitoring.

As organizations embrace multi-cloud architectures, many will continue to support on-premises applications within traditional data centers or private clouds. Protecting these data centers, as well as your multi-cloud environments, requires a comprehensive, consistent security strategy. Consistent security becomes even more powerful when you share threat information across the security infrastructure.

Beyond securing your multi-cloud environments, a comprehensive security platform spans the network and endpoints as well. These security mechanisms — in clouds, networks, and endpoints — essentially act as sensor and enforcement points, working together to arm your business with the collective intelligence required to prevent successful cyberattacks.

# Best Practices for Deployment

For enterprises that use the cloud, the key to being protected starts with understanding the layers that make up the components of their cloud stack (see Figure 2-4). These different layers — services, identity, app edge, load balancer, compute, and storage — create multiple potential targets, and for the informed, each represents a piece of the cloud environment that can be secured against potential threats.

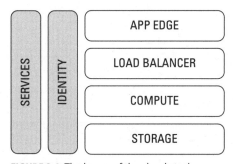

**FIGURE 2-4:** The layers of the cloud stack.

By focusing on the different pieces of the cloud stack and addressing their unique security threats, your environment will be far more resistant to cybersecurity threats. These best practices will help you secure all layers of your stack:

>> **Lock down identity management.** Identity and access management determines what parts of the cloud stack you have access to, and what you can do when you're there. If a bad actor can gain access to your systems using your credentials, you're done. Do the following:

- **Require secure passwords.** Use the longest password or passphrase allowed by the system, or use a complex password that includes a mix of letters, numbers, and symbols.

- **Implement MFA everywhere.** Having a strong password is not enough these days. You need multiple layers of protection. Using a second validation or authentication method provides another layer of protection for your user login.

- **Create least privilege roles.** Only give users access to the least amount of accounts and systems that allow them to be productive. This limits the damage that can be done if a mistake is made or a bad actor gets access to the account.

- **Disable inactive accounts.** When people leave your organization, disable their access to all systems and disable their access keys immediately. Inactive accounts leave more endpoints vulnerable, and account activity is not usually monitored the same as active ones.

- **Monitor for suspicious user behavior or compromised credentials.** Use real-time monitoring that leverages machine learning and analytics to identify suspicious activity and possibly compromised account credentials.

>> **Secure the compute layer.** Take steps to secure your compute layer to ensure availability of systems and data, and to keep bad actors from using your compute power to further spread malware across your business and the Internet. Do the following:

- **Harden the operating system.** Remove unnecessary programs that only serve to broaden your attack surface. Stay up to date on service packs and patches as much as you can. You may still be vulnerable to a zero-day attack, but it makes such an attack much less likely.

- **Continuously check for misconfigurations and anomalies.** Use automated tools to detect changes across the environment, as well as anomalous behavior.

- **Enable secure login.** Issue Secure Shell (SSH) keys to individuals. This will keep your assets protected when moving across unsecured networks.

- **Implement inbound and outbound firewall rules.** Take care to set definitive rules about what, how much, and who can send, receive, and access both inbound and outbound data. Many organizations are reluctant to set up outbound rules, but because attackers will attempt to steal (exfiltrate) your sensitive data and intellectual property, it's important to ensure you have outbound rules that are explicitly defined. These firewall rules need to be created at the Application layer rather than the Transport or Network layer (IP and port information) to prevent attackers from piggybacking off open ports (such as the domain name system [DNS] on port 53).

- **Use only trusted images.** Build your images or templates from scratch or get them from very trusted sources like AWS or Microsoft Azure. Don't use images from Stack Overflow or random message boards and user communities.

» **Secure your storage.** If data is the new oil, you want to be sure to protect your precious resources. If attackers get access to your storage layer, they can potentially delete or expose entire buckets or blobs of data. Do the following:

- **Manage data access.** Identity and access management (IAM) policies and access control lists (ACLs) help you centralize the control of permissions to your storage. Security policies allow you to enable or deny permissions by accounts, users, or based on certain conditions like date, IP address, or whether the request was over a Secure Sockets Layer (SSL) encrypted session.

- **Classify data.** Automatically classify data to ensure you know what type of data is stored and where it's stored. Data classification policies should be matched to security policies, and any violations should be flagged or automatically remediated.

- **Encrypt, encrypt, encrypt.** Encrypt your data both in transit and at rest. Note that the metadata is often not encrypted, so be sure not to store sensitive information in your cloud storage metadata.

- **Enable versioning and logging.** Versioning allows you to preserve, retrieve, and restore data if something goes wrong. With versioning turned on, you can always restore from an older version of the data if a threat or application failure causes loss of data. Maintaining access logs provides an audit trail in case someone or something gets into your system.

- **Do not allow Delete rights (or require MFA for Delete).** You can set up roles in your cloud infrastructure that do not allow users to delete any data. In many cloud storage solutions, you can also enable a feature that requires MFA to delete any version of data stored in your storage layer.

- **Continuously check for misconfigurations and anomalies.** Use automated tools to detect misconfigured storage and permissions settings, as well as anomalous file access behavior.

» **Protect your cloud services.** After you've secured the perimeter and enforced smart policies, you need to focus on security specifically for your services in the cloud. Use source control to secure versions, access to builds, and deployment instances. This will reduce the surface area of your code and limit the potential for attacks across your entire network.

# Chapter **3**

# Looking at Regulatory Compliance in the Cloud

I n this chapter, you learn about select data protection and cyber-security laws relevant to the cloud, the need for automated, continuous compliance monitoring, and how to be proactive in your compliance efforts.

## Navigating the Regulatory Landscape

The regulatory landscape is constantly evolving, with an ever-increasing number of laws and statutes worldwide mandating information security and data protection requirements. Along with more established regulations and standards, such as the U.S. Health Insurance Portability and Accountability Act (HIPAA), U.S. Gramm–Leach–Bliley Act (GLBA), SWIFT data protection policies, Payment Card Industry Data Security Standard (PCI-DSS), and Canada Personal Information Protection and Electronic Documents Act (PIPEDA), recent laws and regulations have garnered much attention, including the European Union's (EU) General Data Protection Regulation (GDPR) and Network and Information Security (NIS) Directive (EU 2016/1148), both of which became enforceable in 2018. These new laws, among others, have important implications for organizations operating in the cloud.

**REMEMBER**

Compliance requirements are typically based on information security best practices, but it's important to remember that security and compliance aren't the same thing.

The GDPR applies to entities that control or process personal data on individuals located in the EU. Personal data is defined in the law quite broadly as any information relating to an individual that is identified or identifiable. In general, this happens in one of the following scenarios:

>> The data identifies or can be used to contact a person (for example, name, email address, date of birth, user ID).

>> The data identifies a unique device (potentially) used by a single person (for example, an IP address or unique device ID).

>> The data reflects or represents a person's behavior or activity (for example, location, applications downloaded, websites visited, and so on).

The GDPR represents a fundamental shift for personal data protection in the EU. It is much stricter than previous data protection laws, with greater scope of coverage — including companies outside the EU — as well as new data breach notification requirements and significant administrative fines.

The GDPR also introduces mandatory notification requirements for breaches of personal data. Supervisory authorities must be informed, in most instances, if personal data is lost, stolen or otherwise compromised without undue delay and, where feasible, not later than 72 hours after having become aware of it. In certain cases, individuals must be notified as well. Notifications must describe a range of details about the breach, such as its nature, categories, and number of personal data records concerned, likely consequences, and measures taken to address the breach and mitigate its effects.

The GDPR also stipulates administrative fines. The consequences of noncompliance (whether egregious or accidental) can be severe: a potential maximum fine of 4 percent of annual global revenue (or maximum €20,000,000, whichever is higher) for noncompliance with its data processing and data management obligations (such as the requirement to get consent, or various rules regarding data transfers to third countries), and 2 percent (or maximum €10,000,000, whichever is higher) for security and data breach notification-related obligations, amongst others.

**WARNING**

The potential reputational harm of data breaches, in addition to the GDPR's mandatory notification mandate, the possibility of regulators' investigations, and significant administrative fines, has firmly placed personal data protection as a board-level concern.

**TIP**

The GDPR is likely to require substantial technology, personnel investments, and business process changes for companies to achieve compliance. The GDPR will impact different groups within an organization, including the legal department, the privacy office, and the chief information security officer (CISO), as well as business teams and product engineers that must implement "privacy by design."

**REMEMBER**

*Privacy by design* means that within the architecture of the application, network, or transport, the organization has taken measures to ensure the privacy of personal data, regardless of the type. To this end, the organization must understand the risks of collecting this information and build their systems with the appropriate security. This represents a shift in thinking for many organizations because they now must integrate security into their design process for architectures that are dealing with any kind of accounts or data. "Privacy by default" is a sister concept to privacy by design in that it accounts for the information that is collected, and how organizations must strive to collect the minimum information necessary and minimize their handling of this data.

The vast majority of GDPR requirements center around data management, namely data collecting and processing. There are obligations to provide notice when collecting personal data, prohibitions of unauthorized data processing, requirements to maintain records of data processing activities, a duty to appoint a data protection officer (DPO) in certain instances, and rules regarding transfer of personal data to third parties and third countries, amongst others.

But this should not overshadow the fact that data security is also a pillar of GDPR. GDPR has specific security-related language, as described in Table 3-1. Plus, a key component of protecting personal data is keeping it secure — both from exfiltration by cyber adversaries and from internal leakage. So, as organizations work toward GDPR compliance, it's imperative that investments in compliance activities and information management processes and technologies be complemented with appropriate investments in cybersecurity.

**TABLE 3-1** Summary of Relevant Provisions from the GDPR

| Topic | Summary of Provisions |
|---|---|
| Security of data processing | Organizations must implement appropriate technical and organizational measures to ensure a level of security appropriate to the risk. Those measures must account for the state of the art. **[Article 32]** |
| | Personal data should be processed in a manner that ensures appropriate security and confidentiality of the data, including for preventing unauthorized access to or use of personal data and the equipment used for the processing. **[Recital, paragraph 39]** |
| | In assessing data security risk, consideration should be given to risks presented by personal data processing. Risks that should be considered include accidental or unlawful destruction, loss, alteration, and unauthorized disclosure of, or access to, personal data. **[Recital, paragraph 83]** |
| Data breach notification | Supervisory authorities must be notified if personal data is lost, stolen, or otherwise compromised, unless the breach is unlikely to result in a relevant risk to the individual. Notification must happen without undue delay and, where feasible, not later than 72 hours after having become aware of the breach. In certain cases, individuals must be notified. Notifications must describe a range of information about the breach, such as its nature, categories and number of personal data records concerned, likely consequences, measures taken to address the breach and mitigate its effects, and other items. **[Articles 33 and 34]** |
| Administrative fines | Supervisory authorities are to impose administrative fines for GDPR infringements, on a case-by-case basis. When deciding whether to impose a fine and the amount, the authorities are directed to consider many factors, including the degree of responsibility in implementing technical and organizational measures, taking into account the state of the art as per Article 32. **[Article 83]** |

TIP

The GDPR calls for technical and organizational security measures that account for the state of the art. Legacy security systems, made up of cobbled-together point products, have proven inadequate to prevent the rising volume, automation, and sophistication of cyberattacks. CISOs should review these legacy products carefully to determine whether they meet the state-of-the-art requirement of the GDPR.

The Network Information and Security (NIS) Directive is the EU's first law specifically focused on cybersecurity. Its goal is to improve the cybersecurity capabilities of the EU critical infrastructure by establishing security and incident notification obligations for various organizations that offer essential and digital services. The NIS Directive also requires member states to enact national cybersecurity strategies and engage in EU cross-border cooperation, among other measures.

Not to be confused with a regulation, the NIS Directive sets out objectives and policies to be attained through legislation at an EU member state level within a certain time frame (a process called *transposition*). Member states were required to transpose the NIS Directive into national law by May 9, 2018.

The NIS Directive requires that Operators of Essential Services (OES) and Digital Service Providers (DSP) use the state-of-the-art technologies to manage risks posed to the security of networks and information systems used to provide the covered services. These entities must also take appropriate measures to prevent and minimize the impact of incidents affecting the security of the networks and information systems that are used to provision essential or digital services, to ensure the continuity of those services. Security incidents of certain magnitude must also be reported to the appropriate national authorities. These obligations apply whether the OES or DSP manages its own network and information systems, or outsources them to the public cloud (for example).

# Recognizing the Importance of Automated, Continuous Monitoring

Security and compliance are shared responsibilities in the public cloud. Many organizations make the mistake of believing that because a public cloud provider manages the security and compliance *of* the cloud, it is also responsible for security and compliance *in* the cloud. That's not the case. It's your data at the end of the day, and if there is a breach or compliance violation, your company will be accountable. The cloud provider delivers a service; the security of your workloads and data is your responsibility as a consumer of the service. It's your revenue, reputation, and customer relationships that are at stake.

A cloud security model should focus on continuous monitoring for, and management of, cloud security risks and threats. Leveraging modern tools and automation techniques to ensure that the organization is aware of and prepared to address vulnerabilities at all times is absolutely essential in the modern threat landscape. This demands the ability to rapidly discover and identify threats in real time; understand their severity; and then immediately act through automated policies, processes, and controls. Point-in-time snapshots of the environment are no longer adequate to ensure protection in the face of dynamic, constantly evolving automated threats.

Organizations must measure security and compliance results constantly, with robust reporting capabilities in the event of an external audit, for example. Achieving this state of continuous security-first compliance requires the use of modern tools and a security platform that leverages the application programming interface (API)–centric architecture of the public cloud.

By using a platform that enables continuous monitoring and management of security in the cloud against policy, IT and security teams will have greater assurance that the organization will be compliant within the required frameworks. Benefits of this model include

>> Compiling a complete unified view across all cloud services

>> Generating compliance reports without the need for specialized knowledge

>> Identifying, prioritizing, and remediating compliance risks as they arise with automation driven by machine learning and analytics — without requiring human interaction

>> Monitoring compliance throughout the entire development life cycle

>> Avoiding "last-minute fire drills" to meet compliance requirements

>> Demonstrating to auditors that the organization is managing security 24/7/365 — not just in the last few weeks before an audit

Compliance and application development teams can both benefit from continuous monitoring and compliance automation. Compliance can significantly reduce time spent on third-party security audits. Application development teams won't get bogged down by compliance audits that stop development projects, thus enabling speed of innovation and development to be competitive differentiators.

TIP

With the right cloud security platform, you can leverage automation to reduce risk and remove the human element from vital processes. This automation allows you to achieve complete and continuous visibility across your cloud deployments, enabling standardized, consistent deployments among usage environments such as development, staging, and production.

# Avoiding the "Compliance Catch-Up" Trap

For many organizations, compliance is a never-ending cycle of audits, reactionary efforts to correct audit discrepancies, and an inevitable drift from the compliant state over time. This "no-win" situation frustrates everyone in the organization and can derail other projects and security initiatives. The speed of deployments and the pace of change in the cloud creates an impossible situation and, frankly, a futile effort for organizations that rely on legacy tools and manual processes to secure their cloud environments and achieve compliance.

Fortunately, new cloud security tools are now available, delivering an agentless platform designed specifically for public clouds and SaaS environments. These solutions leverage the cloud's API to derive tremendous flexibility in scaling and managing cloud security and compliance.

The following steps describe how a modern automated approach to continuous cloud security and compliance works:

>> **Step 1: Monitoring.** The cloud environment is changing continuously. These changes can be normal, routine activities of your DevOps or IT teams; they can also be the work of people who would do harm to your business. As changes are made — across all clouds, regions, and services — the cloud security platform monitors the configurations of the infrastructure to ensure that it adheres to security and compliance best practices.

» **Step 2: Evaluation.** The security platform securely collects data about your cloud services and continuously performs checks against a series of predetermined security best practices and compliance guidelines. It also performs checks against any predefined custom signatures. These checks determine, on a continuous basis, whether there are any potentially exploitable vulnerabilities.

» **Step 3: Deep analysis.** The platform performs an analysis to determine whether the discovered misconfigurations and exposures are ranked as high, medium, or low risk.

» **Step 4: Automated remediation.** The resulting analysis is displayed on a dashboard and predetermined items can be sent to integrated systems for auto-remediation workflows to kick in, when possible and appropriate.

» **Step 5: Robust reporting.** Detailed reports are made available, so your teams can see information about the risk, including user attribution and affected resources. Audit reports from reporting and tracking are also available for compliance efforts.

# FOUR WAYS TO IMPROVE CLOUD SECURITY AND COMPLIANCE

The cloud requires a new way of approaching security. Traditional data center and endpoint security technologies and methodologies are not adequate to protect the highly connected architecture of the cloud. Without a modern, cloud-first approach, security will be compromised because of a variety of factors.

The inherent risk-related challenges can be addressed by employing a security platform built for the cloud that leverages automation to provide continuous monitoring, analysis, prevention, and remediation for cloud security and achieving compliance.

This is a new model that provides comprehensive protection in the cloud. As organizations continue to rely on public cloud to drive day-to-day business activities, as well as innovation, they must reduce security risks and simplify the processes involved in ensuring protection and compliance. Continuous security and compliance present a new opportunity to maximize the value of the public cloud while minimizing risk.

Security experts seek innovative, but usable solutions, and say it is important to focus on four key elements to achieve continuous and automated cloud security and compliance, as follows:

- **Rapid discovery to keep up with the fast pace of change in the cloud:** With the enormity of deployments in the cloud, it isn't unusual for organizations to have millions of data points (such as user or application behavior and configuration settings for cloud services) that need to be evaluated. You need a platform that can handle all the data in real time and rapidly isolate any security variation or deviation from known states.

- **A "single pane of glass" to view your entire cloud environment:** When teams are very large, communication can falter. With each team using different tools to gain a different view of the environment, information becomes siloed and difficult for other teams to understand. Your platform should let teams own their own security, while also providing a "big picture" view to security operations teams and corporate management. The platform must be able to evaluate security data in isolation, as part of the global customer base or across time and geography, to warn about potential issues before they occur.

- **Automated response:** Organizations need to automate not only monitoring and analysis, but also remediation to fix permission or configuration errors. They should have flexibility in determining the course of automated response, with the ability to inform human administrators if there is any other action that may be required.

- **Robust reporting:** Teams need to be able to measure and demonstrate security and compliance progress daily, not just during the yearly audit. With the right platform, you can show your security and compliance posture at the push of a button.

Cloud Security & Compliance For Dummies, Palo Alto Networks Special Edition

# Chapter 4

# Building an Organizational Culture around Security

I n this chapter, you explore the key elements of creating an effective cybersecurity team, how to leverage automation to augment your cybersecurity team, and how to build a secure application development culture within your organization.

## Creating an Effective Cybersecurity Team

Enterprise security isn't easy — and the speed at which enterprises are moving today to innovate and deliver digital services isn't making the challenge any more straightforward. Considering aggressive timetables and delivery deadlines, it's easy to let the discipline required for security slip. But with today's hyper-connected world, and fast-moving and changing cloud environments, letting security slip for even a moment is just something that enterprises simply can't afford. To succeed, enterprises must have the processes and technology — and most certainly the people — in place to keep systems adequately secured.

Creating an effective cybersecurity team begins with an assessment of your organizational needs. This includes identifying teams that may need to be created within the organization (for example, incident response and compliance audit teams), as well as the required skill sets. Next, identify any skills gaps that exist within your current cybersecurity team and determine whether those skills can be attained with training for current team members or whether additional team members need to be hired.

When assessing your organization's cybersecurity needs, remember that automation can enable more rapid response to security incidents by eliminating manual security tasks. Automation thus frees up existing team members to perform other value-added cybersecurity tasks while also limiting the need to hire additional team members. Automation can be a bridge between the shortage of qualified cyber talent in the market and effective cybersecurity.

A recent joint research project by the Enterprise Strategy Group (ESG) and Information Systems Security Association (ISSA) found that 28 percent of cybersecurity professionals and ISSA members feel their organizations depend upon too many manual processes for their day-to-day security operations, such as chasing down data, investigating false positive alerts, or managing remediation tasks. This is exacerbated by a looming shortage of skilled cybersecurity professionals.

There simply aren't enough hours in the day to get to everything, no matter the skill level of your cybersecurity team. With automation, advanced analytics, and security integration, you can begin to bridge the gap. From the cyber defender's perspective, there are three ways to think about automation:

>> **Turn threat detection into prevention.** Organizations shouldn't spend any time manually preventing known threats, because prevention should be automatic. The same goes for unknown threats — they need to be automatically analyzed and blocked if they're malicious.

>> **Adapt to dynamic environments through context-based access policies.** The IT landscape is constantly changing. Security teams must be able to set policies based on the context of what should be protected: users, data, and applications. Context-based policies stand the test of time and adapt to business changes without requiring constant updates.

>> **Automate investigations using analytics and machine learning.** Automation supplies critical leverage, giving organizations an edge over adversaries with insight and context around exploits and techniques. With next-generation firewalls that can ingest third-party data feeds and dynamically update policies, automation turns information into prevention. By using rich security data across locations and deployment types, analytics and machine learning find hidden threats and reconstruct attacks. Both of these automation capabilities save you valuable time.

TIP

A security vendor that offers automation essentially gives you back time to do more valuable, business–critical work. It allows your security teams to move away from basic operational tasks and focus on strategic efforts that directly benefit and improve the security and compliance posture of your organization.

Finally, it's important to know what success looks like for the team. Object key performance indicators (KPIs) should be defined to help the team continuously assess its effectiveness in protecting the organization's cloud assets. Some potential KPIs might include

>> Number and types of security incidents reported

>> SaaS usage, including misconfigurations, accidental sharing, and promiscuous sharing

>> Instances of improperly secured virtual private clouds (VPCs) in Amazon Web Services (AWS) and Google Cloud Platform (GCP), and virtual networks (VNets) in Microsoft Azure

>> Time to detect security breaches

>> Time to remediate breaches and incidents

>> Vulnerabilities identified and patched

>> Threats prevented

# Recognizing How Cloud Maturity Affects Automation Levels

Your organization's cloud maturity (discussed in Chapter 1) largely determines automation levels throughout your environment. Automation can oftentimes be applied to processes throughout the security organization, not just in the cloud. Organizations that already use automation extensively in their cybersecurity processes understand the value of automation in reducing potential configuration errors and enabling rapid security response actions when threats are detected, among others.

For intermediate (cloud implementers) and advanced (cloud optimizers) businesses, automation becomes increasingly important as these organizations increase cloud usage, expand to multi-cloud deployments, and optimize cloud operations. With automation these organizations can successfully scale their cybersecurity operations and reduce the risk of error, allowing them to protect the organization's entire cloud footprint.

REMEMBER

Automation helps secure the business by

>> Creating touchless deployments so that security can be enabled for application development teams and protect the environment from threats without slowing the business

>> Flagging non-compliant services as they're spun up and dynamically updating policies as the environment changes or new threat information is collected

# Embedding Security in the Developer Workflow

Moving at the speed of the cloud raises the concern that costly mistakes could happen. The worry is that as processes are automated, and rapid decisions are made in an environment that prioritizes agility, security compromises will be made. Different stakeholders (such as application development teams and individual business groups), who may not be focused on the broader security picture, now play a more significant role in the cloud conversation. If not properly addressed, unintended consequences — such as security holes due to misconfiguration, choosing "good enough" security, or forgoing security considerations altogether — may ensue.

Compounding this challenge, enterprises face an unprecedented shortage of professionals with cybersecurity skills, especially skills that are critical when it comes to securing DevOps organizations and cloud environments. Consider how much this gap has grown in recent years: A recent survey conducted by Enterprise Strategy Group found that 45 percent of organizations currently report having a "problematic shortage" of cybersecurity skills.

Cloud computing does help to simplify some areas of security, but it doesn't simplify everything. Enterprises are still responsible for the security of their data, applications, operating system, network, firewall configurations, and so on. And although DevOps helps to speed development, it can be challenging to adapt security techniques to keep pace with new application development and deployment capabilities.

TIP

In its October 2017 "10 Things to Get Right for Successful DevSecOps," Gartner wrote, "Don't force information security's old processes to be adopted by DevOps developers. Instead, plan to integrate continuous security assurance seamlessly into the developer's continuous integration/continuous development (CI/CD) toolchain and processes."

So, how can enterprises provide their teams with everything they need to keep their systems secure? It certainly requires having the right technology and processes in place. But getting them in place and keeping them there requires both assembling the right team and making sure everyone on the team does his or her part. But how are these skills cultivated? And how does security become an integral part of the culture of the organization?

The following critical elements will help an enterprise form a smart framework for running a DevOps organization:

> **Continuous cybersecurity skills training and enhancement:** DevOps teams adhere to security best practices, but how those are implemented, and the speed at which they're used must adapt to the speed and agility of a DevOps environment. What does successful implementation of security essentials look like? It's when the entire DevOps team understands security basics including managing secure access to cloud environments, keeping configurations in a secure state, and putting automated controls in place. How is this achieved? Cross-training and more security training. Train operation teams on good security practices, how to use relevant security tools and how to script securely. The same goes for developers who should be continuously trained on secure coding practices to create security champions within the DevOps team. And, above all,

security professionals need to be in continuous contact and collaboration with the rest of the technology teams (for example, development and networking).

REMEMBER

To build a team that can keep systems secure at the speed of DevOps, you need staff that collaborates, understands each other's strengths and weaknesses, helps each other to compensate for those differences, and continuously cross-trains.

» **Security from design through production:** Security efforts should be an integral part of the entire IT process, from the new product, feature, or application design phase through development, application testing, and into production. Too often, security is first addressed during the quality assurance phase or, worse, in production. Staying secure and compliant requires continuous and automated security monitoring of all systems running in production.

REMEMBER

TIP

To properly manage risks, security must be an integral part of the design, development, and production life cycle.

Integrating security processes and built-in security controls into DevOps empowers application development teams with a DevSecOps model that ensures security is properly addressed throughout the application development life cycle.

» **Executive leadership:** Talk with any CIO or CISO about what it takes to build a security-aware DevOps team and the top answer — nearly unanimously — will be that leadership support is the determining factor. Successfully building a secure DevOps organization requires leadership that will help to drive and instill security culture and processes.

» **Automation:** Through automation, you can accomplish two critical prevention-focused tasks:

- You can embed security into your application development workflow, ensuring security keeps pace with development.

- You can ingest external information that can be used to drive/create policies that are dynamically updated as workloads are added or removed from your cloud environment or as new potentially malicious threats are discovered.

REMEMBER

When a process can be automated, it should be automated.

>> **Cultivating the collaborative mind-set:** The spirit of DevOps is to break down the silos in IT departments among developers, operations teams, IT leadership, quality assurance (QA), and security, and embed security as a priority throughout all aspects of development and management. However, for most enterprises, security has been more of a roadblock than an enabler. Communication among security managers and every other team is essential so that everyone comes to understand the roles and challenges of others on the team and identify opportunities to improve. This has always been how the relationship between security and the rest of the IT and development teams should be, but it's especially true for DevOps. Most important to success here is communication and empathy regarding the needs of others. Finally, to foster security collaboration, the right incentives should be in place, such as having security-related KPIs that span multiple teams.

**TIP**

Create an environment where the security team collaborates with other groups and sets incentives to help keep such collaboration aligned.

>> **Security accountability:** If security is to become an integral part of the organization's DevOps culture, the enterprise will need executive leadership that actively shows it cares about security. This way there will be regular, continuous, and comprehensive conversations at all levels of the business regarding aspects of the security program that need to be in place. This is best achieved by having a CISO in place with backing from the board of directors. Engagement helps to create competent security leadership that aligns with DevOps and keeps security efforts synchronized with business needs.

**TIP**

To get the DevOps team and the entire organization aligned when it comes to mitigating business risks, it's crucial to have someone who leads the security efforts.

Cloud Security & Compliance For Dummies, Palo Alto Networks Special Edition

# Chapter **5**

# Forecasting Changes in Cloud Security

n this chapter, you take a glimpse into the future of cloud computing and security.

## Looking at the Direction of Cloud Security

As businesses everywhere continue to migrate their critical applications, workloads, and data to the cloud, public cloud providers will continue to rapidly grow their data center footprints around the world. Data, intellectual property, and compute resources — regardless of their location — are targets for attackers. Hackers' goal is to access the network, navigate to their target, and then execute their attack objectives. The public cloud, by the very nature of its growth and visibility, will be a target-rich environment for attackers for the foreseeable future. Attackers understand the shared responsibility model (discussed in Chapter 1) as well as — or better than — most cloud customers. As such, attackers for the most part will continue to follow the path of least resistance, seeking to exploit the weakest link in an organization's cyber-security chain to gain access to their cloud resources, instead of attempting a direct assault on major public cloud providers such as Amazon, Microsoft, and Google, who themselves invest extensively in cloud security resources.

One trend in cybersecurity that will clearly continue in the future of cloud security is automation. The speed and scale of change makes it impossible for organizations to effectively manage their cybersecurity posture in the cloud with manual tools and processes. Attackers have wholly embraced automation to proliferate malware and brute-force account credentials, among other attack techniques. Cybersecurity teams must respond with automation tools and techniques of their own.

Cloud application architectures will also continue to evolve with practically infinite compute processing resources, increased adoption of containers, new innovations in serverless computing, and more. Extremely large data lakes will also be necessary to handle the deluge of data generated by the Internet of Things (IoT), big and small data analytics, machine learning, and more.

These trends will have security implications themselves, but they'll also impact the technologies used to secure enterprise multi-cloud and on-premises environments of the future. For example, data collection sensors deployed across clouds, users, sites, regions, devices, and so on, will enable ever greater visibility and continuous monitoring across heterogeneous environments. The data generated by these data collection sensors could be hosted as a common data lake of security and threat events, which security vendors can use to build apps or services to add more value and enhance their customers' security and compliance posture.

As artificial intelligence (AI) and machine learning (ML) technologies continue to mature and advance, automation will become more critical in areas such as threat detection and security analysis, particularly given the deluge of sensor data and threat information. Discrete anomalies will increasingly be detected and stopped in real time, effectively closing the window of opportunity for cybercriminals.

# Drafting a Blueprint to Manage Risk

Keep in mind that your move to the cloud means that not only has your risk of breach changed, but you also have increased risk of failure. Developers could take a system down with the click of a button or one wrong line of code in an application deployment. Look to build protections that will reduce security risk and also ensure the availability of critical systems and data. As you rearchitect systems and begin utilizing new technologies and architectures like containers and microservices (or whatever comes next), consider how you'll test to ensure that systems are performing as designed and delivering the expected results.

You need to adapt your existing risk management and cybersecurity frameworks to address the cloud, as well as new and evolving technologies. The NIST Cybersecurity Framework is one example of a great framework to help you get started. The following sections cover the core functions of the framework and how they're affected by your move to the cloud.

## Identify

As you prepare for the future, review your current tool set and skill set to ensure that your team is able to take advantage of new advancements in automated monitoring, detection, reporting, and machine learning. Traditional data center solutions are often unable to keep up with the high volume of data and speed of change. Embed automated security scanning into your DevOps workflows, so that analysis and testing become an integrated part of your development life cycle. To speed adoption, don't make developers learn new tools. Instead, look for tools that support application programming interface (API) enablement and provide rich context.

REMEMBER

If data is the new oil, then machine learning is the new filter that makes it usable by your teams and systems. Leveraging algorithms to discover and classify large amounts of data is a must in the cloud.

# Protect

It used to be that we only had to protect and defend what was inside the perimeter of our data center and our network. However, as organizations move more workloads to SaaS systems and the cloud, network perimeters are expanding and becoming less distinct at an exponential pace. You now need to protect inside your network, across multiple clouds, and out to wherever your mobile users are connecting to the network. Now that the world is your perimeter, you need different means and tools to protect it. Implementing a Zero Trust security model (discussed in Chapter 6) will help set your organization up for success in the cloud.

# Detect

Every organization has been impacted by the shortage in security talent, so it is becoming imperative that organizations of all sizes begin leveraging automation to continuously monitor and analyze events and the effectiveness of deployed controls and protections. Keep in mind that in the cloud, services, virtual machines (VMs), and configurations can change rapidly. In fact, some microservices may exist in your cloud environment for only a few minutes. You must be certain that the tools you employ to detect and log changes can keep pace with these rapid fluctuations.

TIP

Cloud technologies can make certain aspects of the detect function more challenging, but they can also be used to your advantage. Consider using security technologies and services to leverage advanced techniques to detect issues, whether vulnerabilities or attacks, in your networks and systems. Technologies and tools that make use of machine learning to address well-defined security problems, like classifying data for compliance purposes, analyzing and correlating events in log files to find insider threats, or identifying malware and advanced threats across all your endpoints, are just a few examples.

# Respond

When things go wrong, recognize that you need to do more than just stop an attack. You need to know what was impacted, understand what data was accessed, recognize whether there is a compliance impact, and know what your responsibilities are to report the incident.

Today, this function is as much a business response as it is a technical response. Business leaders need to work closely with security and IT teams to ensure that projects are executed within an acceptable level of risk. Response plans need to rise to the level of the board and executive management to ensure they're prepared in the event a major incident impacts the business. Lessons from the Equifax breach or the impact of the Yahoo! breaches on its sale to Verizon are not-so-subtle reminders of how important security and public relations are to the valuation and long-term viability of a business.

As part of your response plan, you can use advanced technologies, such as security tools that streamline the orchestration of threat intelligence and enforcement of prevention-based controls. New tools can remove the manual work of intelligence gathering by allowing you to make use of public, private, and commercial intelligence sources across both government and commercial organizations — and also allow you to share your threat indicators with trusted peers to contribute to global cyber defense efforts. These technologies unify your operational, security, and risk management teams through a single source of truth — the same contextual security data from your modern, advanced systems.

## Recover

For your recovery efforts, it's important to ensure that you have enough information to know what went wrong, so you can fix it — but in cloud environments the amount of data is enormous. Look for tools that will provide you with a single pane of glass for all your event and security logs and will normalize disparate data types so your operational teams can establish a new security baseline. This new security baseline is used to re-evaluate your existing risk framework and suggest possible improvements.

Chapter **6**

# Ten (Or So) Cloud Security Recommendations

In this chapter, I outline some key recommendations to protect data and applications in the cloud.

## Take a Cloud-Centric Approach

The cloud enables your organization to address business challenges with an agile, more scalable approach. To take full advantage of the cloud, recommended best practices include applying the concepts of the modern data center to your cloud deployment architecture, while leaving the traditional constructs behind. In this way, business-critical infrastructure best practices like high availability and scalability can be achieved organically.

# Embrace the Shared Security Model

Public cloud providers, such as Amazon Web Services (AWS), Google Cloud Platform (GCP), and Microsoft Azure, make it clear that security is a shared responsibility. In this model, the provider is responsible for ensuring the platform is always on, available, and up to date.

In fact, the cloud provider's global data center infrastructure is more secure than most organizations' own data centers. However, you, the customer, are responsible for protecting your own applications and data running within the public cloud.

Figure 6-1 highlights the responsibility breakdown. You're in complete control of what security to implement and must take steps to safeguard your content, be that customer data or intellectual property. The benefit of embracing the shared security model is that your team is focused on protecting your apps and data, typically your most valuable assets.

**Public Cloud Security Responsibility**

| | |
|---|---|
| **Security is on you** | Applications (including operating system) and associated data deployed |
| | Account controls (access control, services enabled, and so on) |
| | Deployment architecture, configuration management, and so on |
| **Security is on the provider** | Worldwide footprint (regional presence and so on) |
| | Physical components (buildings, server hardware, resiliency, and so on) |
| | Compute infrastructure (network, database, storage, and so on) |

**FIGURE 6-1:** Public cloud shared responsibility model.

# Use a Zero Trust Strategy

What happens when you ink a deal with a public cloud or web service is what is known as the "uneven handshake." The vendor agrees to provide you with an array of services, but it doesn't assume responsibility for managing your cyber risk. Instead, the vendor provides you with a number of options for how you might set up and configure its security tools.

Traditional, perimeter-centric security strategies fail to provide adequate visibility, control, and protection of user and application traffic. Zero Trust architectures apply the principle of "never trust, always verify" to all entities — users, devices, applications, and packets — regardless of what they are *or* their location relative to the bounds of the corporate network (see Figure 6-2).

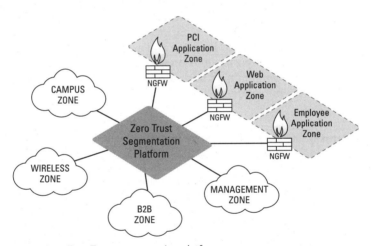

**FIGURE 6-2:** Zero Trust segmentation platform.

When enterprise leaders are thinking about entering into a cloud agreement, it's critical that they start thinking about a security model for protecting the digital business. What's more, because most companies are in multiple cloud environments, they must be able to put in place and oversee a strategy that encompasses multiple platforms in multiple locations, where regulations can vary dramatically.

By establishing Zero Trust boundaries—just as they would to effectively compartmentalize different segments of their own networks—companies can better protect critical data hosted in the cloud from unauthorized applications or users, reduce the exposure of vulnerable systems, and prevent the movement of malware throughout their network.

# Engage with Business Groups, Governance, and DevOps Early

Most cloud projects are driven by business groups and managed by DevOps teams. Quickly spinning up new products or functional prototypes is commonplace and can happen with only a few hours of notice. A common challenge is that the security team is often brought in to review the architecture after the workload is already running in the cloud. By including security and governance earlier in the process, business and architecture decisions will be made with a security-first approach. This greatly reduces the burden of maintaining a secure environment and achieving compliance when required.

# Know Your Potential Exposure

Public cloud usage is prolific due to the ease of spinning up compute and storage resources. Employees doing what is "right for the business right now" versus what is "right for the business" may create security holes if the environment is not configured properly. It's imperative to know who in your organization is using the cloud and to ensure the environment is configured correctly. To reduce cloud risk, you should do the following:

>> **Monitor cloud usage.** Perhaps the quickest way to determine usage is to look at how much your organization is spending in AWS, GCP, and/or Microsoft Azure.

>> **Ensure proper configuration.** Configure the environment with security best practices in mind. Establish secure defaults

for identity and resource access, enable all audit and security logging capabilities, and properly segment workloads into dedicated environments. This gives you a secure baseline from which to implement workload-specific configurations.

>> **Require multi-factor authentication (MFA).** To minimize the risk of an attacker gaining access using stolen credentials, MFA should be required. Using intelligent challenge-response mechanisms can also protect apps in the cloud from unauthorized access.

>> **Lock down administrative interfaces.** For example, Secure Shell (SSH) on port 22 is a preferred method to securely manage cloud servers, yet it's often left exposed in AWS, GCP, and Microsoft Azure environments for convenience. Other administrative ports, including those for container management systems, application admin consoles, and other similar interfaces should be strictly controlled and protected.

# Understand the Attacker

Attackers leverage automation to find potential targets within minutes. When they've identified those targets, they look for weaknesses, checking default passwords, probing for SSH misconfigurations, and so on.

To highlight the effects of attackers' automation capabilities, Palo Alto Networks spun up a test environment with a database and a web server in the public cloud to demonstrate the extent of attackers' capabilities. The environment was probed from more than 35 countries with more than 25 different attacker applications. In Palo Alto Networks' research efforts, a full global scan of all AWS, Azure, and Google Cloud servers took 23 minutes to complete and revealed tens of thousands of exposed systems. Unlike in a private data center, where there is less concern about public exposure, resources in the public cloud are widely exposed and should be handled carefully.

# Evaluate Your Security and Compliance Options

There are several security options to choose from when moving to the cloud, most of which are like the options for physical networks, including the following:

>> **Native security services:** Cloud service providers offer native security services including security groups, web application firewalls (WAFs), configuration monitoring, and many more. These tools are a good starting point for those without added security technologies, but the capabilities should be supplemented with enterprise-grade security offerings. The following two examples highlight the need for third-party security tools:

- **Security groups** and port-based firewalls are essentially port-based access control lists, providing filtering capabilities. They cannot identify applications by content, and you won't be able to prevent threats or, more important, stop outbound data exfiltration like a next-generation firewall can.

- **WAFs** are limited because they can only protect HTTP and HTTPS applications. This means that WAFs can't protect applications that may use a wide range of ports to function properly. Plus, they aren't an effective means of identifying and controlling remote management or access tools, such as SSH or Microsoft Remote Desktop Protocol (RDP).

>> **Point products:** Organizations that deploy point products that are designed to solve a particular use case end up deploying numerous products from different security vendors. This creates complexity with a fragmented set of security tools that don't seamlessly integrate and communicate with each other, and require specialized skills to operate and manage. Automation becomes difficult, if not impossible to achieve.

>> **Do-it-yourself (DIY) security:** Some organizations choose a DIY approach to securing cloud workloads, using custom scripts and open-source projects to protect deployments. Disadvantages to this strategy include the burden of improving custom tools, lack of expertise to manage the

security implementation and operations, and nonexistent support in the event of a security breach.

Organizations that rely on internal personnel to manage cloud and security deployments must be prepared for attrition. Typically, only a few engineers know the environment well, but they don't necessarily have time to keep proper documentation or manage knowledge-sharing requirements. If even one of those engineers leaves the company, the organization may not be well positioned to effectively manage security — particularly DIY security — needs moving forward.

>> **Security platforms:** The goal for many organizations is to eliminate a fragmented security approach where the security tools don't communicate with each other to successfully prevent attacks. To overcome this challenge, organizations typically adopt a security strategy that utilizes a platform approach. This approach delivers security through in-line, application programming interface (API)–based and host-based protection technologies working together to minimize attack opportunities:

- Secure in-line traffic provides inbound and outbound protections, segmentation of workloads, and threat prevention capabilities.

- Monitor and protect public cloud resources via cloud provider APIs. These resources need to be monitored continuously rather than through point-in-time checks.

- Maintain the integrity of the operating system and applications on the virtual workloads blocking exploits, ransomware, malware, and fileless attacks.

# Empower Yourself with Knowledge

Personal branding consultant John Antonios once said, "Knowledge plus action is power." In cloud security, knowledge begins with ingesting large sets of data produced by the cloud, network, and endpoints. This data then needs to be analyzed to find the threats that need to be acted on to protect your cloud.

Security tools need to be able to share this threat information with other parts of the cloud, points of enforcement, and the broader enterprise-wide IT deployment. Then, to help fight large-scale attacks and ensure future detection of similar attacks, this information needs to be shared with the broader community and security industry.

Attackers must then develop new tools, acquire new infrastructure, or develop different attack techniques from the ones already exposed. These changes require time, money, and other resources, which increase the cost to conduct the attack.

As you build your cloud security strategy for your environment, ensure that your security tools are capable of sharing threat intelligence across your broader enterprise and receiving threat data from external sources.

**TIP**

To fast-track secure cloud adoption, consult cloud security experts through communities or vendors. The guidance will ensure you build the right security foundation to enable your business in the cloud.

# Believe in Prevention

There are those who believe the attackers have already "won," and thus choose to focus primarily on a detection and remediation approach. However, a prevention philosophy is critical to dealing with the volume of threats. Strong prevention minimizes the number of events that require detection and response, allowing you to rapidly stop sophisticated attacks before they can steal confidential data. Enabling the prevention of successful cyberattacks in the cloud requires four key capabilities:

>> **Complete visibility:** The combination of knowledge and enforcement is a powerful security tool. It's critical to identify all your cloud resources, ongoing cloud activity, relative risk tied to current security measures, and any changes to your environment. With this knowledge, a more consistent security policy can be deployed globally to protect your cloud from known and unknown attacks.

**TIP**

Legacy security tools and techniques designed for traditional data centers must transform to be relevant in the cloud. New security capabilities are required to integrate with cloud services. For a complete perspective, ensure that your security tools give you full visibility into IaaS, PaaS, and SaaS resources.

>> **Reduce opportunities for attack.** Using a Zero Trust (never trust, always verify) security approach and application identity as a means of enforcing a positive security model reduces the opportunity for attack by enabling only allowed applications and denying all else. You can align application usage to business needs, control application functions, and stop threats from gaining access and moving laterally within your cloud and network infrastructure.

>> **Prevent known threats.** Leveraging globally shared threat intelligence to apply threat prevention policies is a key step in adhering to a prevention philosophy. These threat prevention policies can block known threats, including vulnerability exploits, malware, and malware-generated command-and-control traffic.

>> **Prevent unknown threats.** Unknown and potentially malicious files must be analyzed based on hundreds of behaviors. If a file is deemed malicious, a prevention mechanism should be delivered quickly and automatically. The information gained from file analysis can then be used to continually improve all other prevention capabilities.

# Secure IaaS and PaaS

Development teams and cloud administrators are responsible for ensuring their data and applications are secure, as defined in the shared responsibility model. Here are some specific critical steps you should take to ensure that you're doing your part:

>> **Disable root account API access keys.** A "root" user is the login credential you used to create your cloud account. Best practices recommend that the root user is only used to create your initial administrative accounts. All future administration should then be completed through newly created identity and access management (IAM) accounts.

» **Enable multi-factor authentication (MFA) tokens everywhere.** MFA should be required of all users, both inside and outside your organization.

» **Follow the principle of least privilege.** J.H. Saltzer described it best: Every program and every user of the system should operate using the least set of privileges necessary to complete the job.

» **Reduce the number of users with admin rights.** The more granular you are with access to your cloud accounts, the more you help protect your business if and when something is compromised.

» **Rotate all keys regularly.** Credentials, passwords, and API access keys should all be rotated on a regular basis. If a credential is compromised, this limits the amount of time that a key is valid.

» **Do not allow 0.0.0.0/0 unless you mean it.** Allowing traffic from 0.0.0.0/0 means that every machine, everywhere can make a connection to your cloud resources — and this also means that your systems can make outbound connections to every system, everywhere. Instead, use security groups and network access control lists to limit both inbound and outbound traffic.

» **Turn on logging everywhere.** Too often, activity logging in cloud environments is turned off, or never turned on. Without logs, how will you ever know if your environment has been breached?

» **Turn on encryption.** Make sure your data is encrypted from the start. It is much more challenging to go back and sort through data to try and re-encrypt it after the fact. Much like enabling the service itself, this will help keep your data secure.

# Use Automation to Eliminate Bottlenecks

Automation is a central tenet of the public cloud, where rapid change is constant. When security best practice change control is followed, the delay may introduce friction, slowing deployments or, worse, weakening security if the deployment does not "wait" for change control to work. Here are two automation tool sets that can help organizations eliminate security-induced friction and take advantage of the flexibility and agility benefits offered in the public cloud:

>> Automated deployment systems and orchestration frameworks that enable security infrastructure to be deployed "as code" in a seamless and touchless manner.

>> Automation tools that use continuous monitoring, data analytics, and enforcement to respond more quickly to the ever-changing threat landscape.

Cloud Security & Compliance For Dummies, Palo Alto Networks Special Edition

# Glossary

**access control list (ACL):** A list of rights and permissions assigned to a subject for a given object.

**ACL:** *See* access control list.

**adware:** Pop-up advertising programs that are commonly installed with freeware or shareware. *See also* malware.

**anti-AV software:** Malware that disables any legitimately installed antivirus software on a compromised endpoint, thereby preventing automatic detection and removal of malware that is subsequently installed by the attacker. Many anti-AV programs work by infecting the master boot record (MBR) of a target endpoint. *See also* malware.

**API:** *See* application programming interface.

**application programming interface (API):** A set of protocols, routines, and tools used to develop and integrate applications.

**backdoor:** Malware that enables an attacker to bypass normal authentication procedures in order to gain access to a compromised system and is often installed as a failover, in case other malware is detected and removed from the system. *See also* malware.

**bootkit:** A kernel-mode variant of a rootkit, commonly used to attack computers that are protected by full-disk encryption. *See also* malware.

**bot:** An individual endpoint that has been infected with malware. *See also* botnet *and* malware.

**botnet:** A network of bots working together and controlled by an attacker through command-and-control servers. *See also* bot *and* malware.

**CASB:** *See* cloud access security broker.

**Chef:** A software management tool that automates infrastructure configuration, deployment, and management as code.

**cloud access security broker (CASB):** A software tool or service that enforces an organization's security policies between users of cloud services and the cloud service providers, including IaaS, PaaS, and SaaS providers.

**Cloud Security Alliance Cloud Controls Matrix (CSA CCM):** A control framework, consisting of 16 domains, which describes cloud security principles and best practices and provides guidance to help organizations assess the overall security risk of a cloud provider.

**community cloud:** A cloud computing deployment model that consists of a cloud infrastructure that is used exclusively by a specific group of organizations.

**Computer Security Incident Response Team (CSIRT):** A team that is designated to respond to security incidents, including investigation, remediation, and recovery.

**container:** A self-contained packaging mechanism in which an instance of an application can run a specific task or code.

**CSA CCM:** *See* Cloud Security Alliance Cloud Controls Matrix.

**CSIRT:** *See* Computer Security Incident Response Team.

**DevOps:** A software engineering approach that promotes greater collaboration between software development and IT operations to promote business agility.

**DevSecOps:** The integration of security practices with DevOps. *See also* DevOps.

**DNS:** *See* Domain Name System.

**Docker:** A popular containerization program. *See also* container.

**Domain Name System (DNS):** A hierarchical, decentralized directory service database that converts domain names to IP addresses for computers, services, and other computing resources connected to a network or the Internet.

**ENISA:** *See* European Union Agency for Network and Information Security.

**European Union Agency for Network and Information Security (ENISA):** A decentralized agency of the European Union created in 2004 to improve network and information security in the EU.

**exploit:** Software or code that takes advantage of a vulnerability in an operating system or application, and causes unintended behavior in the operating system or application, such as privilege escalation, remote control, or a denial-of-service.

**Extensible Markup Language (XML):** A human- and machine-readable markup language.

**GDPR:** *See* General Data Protection Regulation.

**General Data Protection Regulation (GDPR):** A European Union regulation on data protection and privacy for all individuals within the EU and the European Economic Area. The GDPR supersedes the Data Protection Directive (95/46/EC) and became enforceable in 2018.

**Health Insurance Portability and Accountability Act (HIPAA):** U.S. legislation passed in 1996 that, among other things, protects the confidentiality and privacy of protected health information (PHI). *See also* protected health information.

**HIPAA:** *See* Health Insurance Portability and Accountability Act.

**HTTP:** *See* Hypertext Transfer Protocol.

**HTTP Secure (HTTPS):** Also referred to as HTTP over SSL/TLS. The HTTP protocol encrypted with SSL or TLS. *See also* Hypertext Transfer Protocol *and* Secure Sockets Layer/Transport Layer Security.

**HTTPS:** *See* HTTP Secure.

**hybrid cloud:** A cloud computing deployment model that is composed of public and private cloud infrastructures.

**Hypertext Transfer Protocol (HTTP):** An application protocol used to transfer data between web servers and web browsers.

**IaaS:** *See* Infrastructure as a Service.

**IAM:** *See* identity and access management.

**identity and access management (IAM):** The processes and procedures that support the life cycle of people's identities and access privileges in an organization.

**IDS:** *See* intrusion detection system.

**IETF:** *See* Internet Engineering Task Force.

**Infrastructure as a Service (IaaS):** A category of cloud computing services in which the customer manages operating systems, applications, compute, storage, and networking, but the underlying physical cloud infrastructure is maintained by the service provider.

**Internet Engineering Task Force (IETF):** An international, membership-based, nonprofit organization that develops and promotes voluntary Internet standards.

**International Organization for Standardization (ISO):** An international standard-setting body composed of representatives from various national standards organizations.

**Internet Protocol Security (IPsec):** An IETF open-standard VPN protocol for secure communications over IP-based public and private networks. *See also* Internet Engineering Task Force *and* virtual private network.

**intrusion detection system (IDS):** A hardware or software application that detects and logs suspected network or host intrusions.

**intrusion prevention system (IPS):** A hardware or software application that both detects and blocks suspected network or host intrusions.

**IPS:** *See* intrusion prevention system.

**IPsec:** *See* Internet Protocol Security.

**ISO:** *See* International Organization for Standardization.

**jump host:** A secure, isolated computer on a network that is used exclusively to perform privileged administrative functions on the network.

**Kubernetes:** A popular open-source container orchestration program used for automating the deployment, scaling, and management of containerized applications. *See also* container.

**least privilege:** A principle requiring that a subject is granted only the minimum privileges necessary to perform an assigned task.

**logic bomb:** A program, or portion thereof, designed to perform some malicious function when a predetermined circumstance occurs. *See also* malware.

**malware:** Malicious software or code that typically damages or disables, takes control of, or steals information from a computer system. Malware broadly includes adware, anti-AV software, backdoors, bootkits, bots and botnets, logic bombs, RATs, rootkits, spyware, Trojan horses, viruses, and worms.

**MFA:** *See* multi-factor authentication.

**microservices:** A collection of loosely coupled services that comprise an application.

**multi-factor authentication (MFA):** An authentication mechanism that requires two or more of the following factors: something you know, something you have, something you are.

**National Institute of Standards and Technology (NIST):** The U.S. federal agency that is responsible for working with industry to develop and apply technology, measurements, and standards.

**NetBIOS:** A service that enables applications on separate computers to communicate over a local area network.

**Network and Information Security (NIS) Directive:** A European Union directive passed in 2016 to create an overall higher level of cybersecurity in the EU, particularly among digital service providers (DSPs) and operators of essential services (OESs).

**NIS:** *See* Network and Information Security (NIS) Directive.

**NIST:** *See* National Institute of Standards and Technology.

**PaaS:** *See* Platform as a Service.

**Payment Card Industry Data Security Standard (PCI DSS):** A proprietary information security standard mandated for organizations that handle American Express, Discover, JCB, MasterCard, or Visa payment cards.

**PCI DSS:** *See* Payment Card Industry Data Security Standard.

**Personal Information Protection and Electronic Documents Act (PIPEDA):** A Canadian data privacy law that governs how private sector organizations collect, use, and disclose personal information in the course of commercial business.

**PHI:** *See* protected health information (PHI).

**PIPEDA:** *See* Personal Information Protection and Electronic Documents Act.

**Platform as a Service (PaaS):** A category of cloud computing services in which the customer is provided access to a platform for deploying applications and can manage limited configuration settings, but the operating system, compute, storage, networking, and underlying physical cloud infrastructure are maintained by the service provider.

**private cloud:** A cloud computing deployment model that consists of a cloud infrastructure that is used exclusively by a single organization.

**protected health information (PHI):** Any information about health status, healthcare, or healthcare payments that can be associated with a specific, identifiable individual.

**public cloud:** A cloud computing deployment model that consists of a cloud infrastructure that is open to use by the general public.

**Puppet:** A software management tool that automates infrastructure configuration, deployment, and management as code.

**RAT:** *See* remote access Trojan.

**RDP:** *See* Remote Desktop Protocol.

**remote access Trojan (RAT):** A malware program that includes a backdoor to provide administrative control of a target computer. *See also* malware.

**Remote Desktop Protocol (RDP):** A proprietary Microsoft protocol that provides remote access to a computer. RDP uses TCP port 3389 and UDP port 3389 by default.

**rootkit:** Malware that provides privileged (root-level) access to a computer. *See also* malware.

**SaaS:** *See* Software as a Service.

**Secure Shell (SSH):** A cryptographic network protocol that provides secure access to a remote computer.

**Secure Sockets Layer/Transport Layer Security (SSL/TLS):** A transport layer protocol that provides session-based encryption and authentication for secure communication between clients and servers on the Internet.

**serverless computing:** A cloud computing execution model in which the cloud provider dynamically manages the allocation of server resources.

**Service Organization Control (SOC) 2:** An audit report, defined by the American Institute of Certified Public Accountants (AICPA), that focuses on controls (that are not specifically related to internal controls over financial reporting) at a service organization relevant to security, availability, processing integrity, confidentiality, and privacy.

**shadow IT:** IT applications and services that are acquired and operated by end users without explicit organizational approval and often without organizational IT knowledge or support.

**shared responsibility model:** A cloud security framework that defines the security responsibilities of the cloud provider and its customers within different service delivery models (such as IaaS, PaaS, and SaaS) for various aspects of the environment such as data, application, compute, and data center security. See also Infrastructure as a Service (IaaS), Platform as a Service (PaaS), and Software as a Service (SaaS).

**SOC 2:** *See* Service Organization Control (SOC) 2.

**Software as a Service (SaaS):** A category of cloud computing services in which the customer is provided access to a hosted application that is maintained by the service provider.

**spyware:** Software that gathers information about a person or organization without their knowledge or consent. *See also* malware.

**SSH:** *See* Secure Shell.

**SSL/TLS:** *See* Secure Sockets Layer/Transport Layer Security.

**TCP:** *See* Transmission Control Protocol.

**Transmission Control Protocol (TCP):** A connection-oriented protocol responsible for establishing a connection between two hosts and guaranteeing the delivery of data and packets in the correct order.

**Trojan horse:** A program that purports to perform a given function, but that actually performs some other (usually malicious) function. *See also* malware.

**Uniform Resource Locator (URL):** Commonly known as a "web address." The unique identifier for any resource connected to the web.

**URL:** *See* Uniform Resource Locator.

**virtual network (VNet):** An on-demand pool of shared computing resources allocated within Azure cloud.

**virtual private cloud (VPC):** An on-demand pool of shared computing resources allocated within Amazon Web Services or Google Cloud Platform.

**virtual private network (VPN):** An encrypted tunnel that extends a private network over a public network (such as the Internet).

**virus:** A set of computer instructions whose purpose is to embed itself within another computer program in order to replicate itself. *See also* malware.

**VNet:** *See* virtual network.

**VPC:** *See* virtual private cloud.

**VPN:** *See* virtual private network.

**vulnerability:** A bug or flaw in software that creates a security risk that may be exploited by an attacker.

**WAF:** *See* web application firewall.

**web application firewall (WAF):** A device used to protect a web server from web application attacks such as script injection and buffer overflow.

**worm:** Malware that usually has the capability to replicate itself from computer to computer without the need for human interaction. *See also* malware.

**XML:** *See* Extensible Markup Language.